Jesus AND Lao Tzu

THE PARALLEL SAYINGS

D0858757

Jesus AND Lao Tzu

THE PARALLEL SAYINGS

with Commentaries

EDITOR

Martin Aronson

INTRODUCTION

David Steindl-Rast

Seastone

BERKELEY, CALIFORNIA

First Ulysses Press Edition 2000

Published by:
Seastone, an imprint of Ulysses Press
P.O. Box 3440
Berkeley, CA 94703
www.ulyssespress.com

Library of Congress Cataloging-in-Publication Data

Jesus and Lao Tzu: the parallel sayings / editor, Martin Aronson; introduction,
David Steindl-Rast
      p. cm.
    ISBN 1-56975-224-9 (paper : alk. paper)
    I. Jesus Christ--Teachings. 2. Lao-tzu. Tao te ching. 3. Taoism Sacred books--
Quotations. I. Aronson, Martin, 1953-
BS2415.A3 J47 2000
232.9'54--dc21   00-064902
                                                  CIP

ISBN 1-56975-319-9 (paperback)

Printed in Canada by Transcontinental Printing

10 9 8 7 6 5 4 3 2 1

Editorial and production: Steven Schwartz, Marin Van Young, Lynette Ubois
Design: Leslie Henriques and Big Fish
Cover art: *Deesis Christ with St. John the Baptist* (detail), Hagia Sophia, Istanbul, Turkey/Bridgeman Art Library; *Lao Tse, 2nd of the "Three Pure Ones*," Marburg, Germany, Foto Marburg/Art Resource, NY

Distributed in the United States by Publishers Group West and in Canada by Raincoast Books

CONTENTS

PREFACE

by Brother David Steindl-Rast, O.S.B.

The snow-capped peaks near the St. Gotthard Pass in Switzerland are the headwater region of both Rhine and Rhone. Here, high up in the Swiss Alps, these twin rivers gush forth less than twenty miles apart. One will flow north, one south, till the whole width of Europe lies between their mouths. Could a French child splashing about in the Mediterranean at the mouth of the Rhone and a Dutch child wading in the North Sea by the mouth of the Rhine ever surmise their connection? Thousands of miles apart they are dipping into the same waters, waters that flow from mountain peaks that neither of them has ever seen.

The two rivers from which Martin Aronson has scooped up the parallel sayings in this book are not at all parallel rivers. Taoist tradition and Christian tradition do not run parallel; they are more divergent still than Rhine and Rhone. The vastly different landscapes they flow through have less in common than Geneva and Constance, Lyons and Strasbourg, Avignon and Cologne. The distinct cultural and linguistic landscapes along the embankments of our two traditions are mirrored in their waters and make the two on the surface utterly dissimilar. These important and yet superficial differences make the deep similarities between them all the more striking. Taoist and Christian waters flow down from the same mountains and have their origin in the same eternal snows.

What shall we call that hidden source whose taste we can discern in the sayings presented in this book? Maybe we could call it Common Sense. Unfortunately, this fine term has fallen on hard times. To most people it suggests no more than sweet reason, levelheadedness, or horse sense. But Common Sense deserves to be restored to its full meaning. It points toward that mystical wellspring of spiritual aliveness which is common to all humans and which alone can make us see sense. We need a term to express just this notion in contemporary English. Having a name for it might help us appreciate what the name expresses. Appreciation, in turn, will help us live by Common Sense.

It has happened before that an everyday term, worth no more than a pebble, was picked up, polished, and given the setting of a jewel. Heraclitus did this with the word Logos, which before him meant no more than "thought," or "word." Lao Tzu's term, Tao, meant no more than "road," or "way," until he made it stand for the same mysterious wellspring that Logos attempted to name. Logos and Tao are not words that belong to our living language, but if we know what they want to convey we will find it there, close to home, in the deepest meaning of our own term Common Sense.

"Nothing is less common than Common Sense," the early-20th-century English writer G. K. Chesterton quipped. He was partially right: not that we don't all have Common Sense, but we do not commonly live by it. That's why our lives don't make sense. And this is precisely what both Lao Tzu and Jesus point out to us. Neither of them declares with great fanfare truths that no one has ever heard before. On the contrary, "Who of you doesn't know this?" they ask teasingly. And when we have to admit, "Well, everyone knows this," they laugh: "Then why don't you live accordingly?" We have fallen into their trap. It was a joke, albeit a serious one, and we are invited to have a good laugh at ourselves.

The parables of Jesus, his typical form of teaching, are jokes of this kind. The joke is on us (all the more so the less we are aware of it). "Who of you doesn't know this already?" Jesus asks time and again. Who of you doesn't know who your neighbor is when you are in trouble? Of course, anyone who comes along should act neighborly when *I* need help. Why not remember this when *they* are in trouble and you come along. Or who of you will stay unforgiving when your wayward child comes home in rags? Well then, do you think God will? Or who of you will pull up the wheat along with the weeds? For heaven's sakes, use Common Sense!

Lao Tzu is using Common Sense when he observes that water, the life-giving element, always flows down to the lowest level; that even the strongest rock cannot resist the power of weak water. This implies the hope that Common Sense will be a strong enough current to undermine our hard-as-rock consensus reality. One day all our phoniness will come tumbling down in a great peal of laughter, just as when the child at the parade cried out, "But the emperor isn't wearing any clothes at all!"

The names of Rhine and Rhone differ only by one letter. Their basic significance is the same, namely, "the flow." To stay in the Tao, in the Logos, in Common Sense, means to stay in the flow. The Rhine and Rhone have also this in common: Just before they leave the Alps, the region of their common beginnings, each of them pauses and gathers its waters in a splendid lake—the Rhone in the Lake of Geneva, the Rhine in the Lake of Constance. The Gospels and the Tao Te Ching resemble two lakes of this kind. Our two traditions find in them the waters of their beginnings splendidly gathered before they flow out into world history. So dazzling is the sight of these lakes that we might be tempted to lose ourselves in mere looking, but this would be to miss the point. No matter how still the lakes, their waters keep flowing. To get into this flow is the point; it is also the message of the book you hold in your hands.

Martin Aronson, who compiled these parallel sayings of Lao Tzu and Jesus, tells us "an organic unity between them seeped into [his] soul," as he pored over these texts. In this seepage we recognize the groundwater of Common Sense. We find it distilled in Perennial Wisdom, but we find it also rising up from the depth of our own souls. "When we see deeply into the fabric of reality," Martin Aronson reminds us, "we glimpse the unity behind the diversity." In these moments, we find sense and meaning in life, we find life's significance—not as superimposed on the fabric of reality, but as our sense of belonging to it. Common Sense is our awareness of being inextricably interwoven in the fabric of reality. But this sounds too dry for a fabric woven of damp roots, dewy tendrils, moist filaments. What we find as we go deep is humid; it is the stuff of humility, humor, and humanness—that of Lao Tzu, of Jesus, and of our own common humanity. Like water, it rises, gathers and flows.

In the Tao, the Logos, in Common Sense, flows our only hope. Nothing holds greater promise for the future because nothing is more subversive. Common Sense is subversive because sooner or later it brings down everything that offends against our common humanity and our cosmic community, all that is so widely accepted though it may not make sense. Nonviolently subversive Common Sense, like the steady drip that wears down rock, underwashes all walls of division and makes them fall. But, above all, it irrigates, makes grow, renews. We must be renewed from this source. To those who have ears to hear, every page of this book proclaims in its two voices one and the same message: Drink from this living water, dive into it, flow with it, come alive, live!

Differing Lives, Parallel Sayings

For two great religious figures, founders of two of the world's great spiritual traditions, it is hard to imagine how the lives of Lao Tzu and Jesus could have been more different. Although our knowledge of both is limited at best, what we do know points to two strikingly different life journeys.

Jesus, as nearly everyone on the planet knows, was born in Palestine 2000 years ago in the age of the Roman Empire, began his ministry around age 30, preached his message of love and social justice for approximately three years, and was executed by the agonizing Roman method of crucifixion. Lao Tzu, on the other hand, in the bare bones legend of his life that is all we have been handed down, lived a simple, quiet life as keeper of the imperial archives in his native western Chinese state of K'uhsien about five centuries before Jesus was born. Legend claims he was an older contemporary of Confucius—who purportedly left an account of meeting Lao Tzu, in which Confucius likened Lao Tzu's mysterious presence to that of a dragon.

Apparently deeply disenchanted with the strife and artificiality of civilization, Lao Tzu retired from his position sometime in middle to late life, renounced society, and mounted a water buffalo to ride west toward Tibet, where he would live in solitude. At the Hankao Pass, a gatekeeper tried to talk him out of becoming a hermit in his old age and asked him to turn back. Lao Tzu refused. The gatekeeper then asked him to at least write down his thoughts before he abandoned civilization, and this Lao Tzu agreed to do. According to the legend, Lao Tzu returned three days later with his little jewel of a book, the Tao Te Ching, "The Way and Its Power." Then he passed beyond the gate and was never heard from again.

So there you have lives of profound contrast: Jesus was an impassioned prophet and engaged social reformer who made a heroic effort to transform society and indeed perhaps all of humanity, and died young and painfully for his efforts. Lao Tzu preached to no one (not even the gatekeeper), amassed no followers in his lifetime, founded no church, lived quietly and inconspicuously almost his entire long life of more than 80 years, and ultimately turned his back on society to live a life of peace and contemplation, close to nature, in his final years.

Yet even in the stark contrast of the outlines of these two lives, if we look close enough, we can see some parallels—slim as they may be. For one, some scholars doubt either one ever existed, claiming that both are legendary, mythological figures whose words are later compilations of many writers and editors. But this point of view is not accepted by most scholars, who maintain that the words and messages, in large part at least, have the coherence and tone of single extraordinary figures. Another is that great mythologies arose about the two figures in the religious traditions that grew around them—in Jesus' case, the doctrines of his Pre-existence, his Virgin Birth, and the Trinity. In Lao Tzu's case, amazing stories that he was conceived of a shooting star and carried by his mother for 82 years until he was born a wise old man with white hair were popular. Such mythologies, if nothing else, attest to the power of the two sages over their followers, the uniqueness of their characters, and the depth of their teachings.

On a more realistic level, we might note that in their lives, despite Jesus' short period of notoriety, both exhibited a profound predilection for anonymity and simplicity, and both philosopher sages remained largely unfettered to the prosaic social world and all its cares and responsibilities. In the broadest blanket, and in the spirit of paradox that both were so fond of employing, we can say that Jesus and Lao Tzu were both simple, humble men of profound mystery and brilliance.

Since their life experiences were so divergent, we are left with the question of how their messages could be so similar. Jesus grew up in the relative (if restless) calm of the Pax Romana, while Lao Tzu lived through the debilitating "period of contending states" in which China was torn almost continuously by war and social chaos. Yet both deplored violence and the use of force. Opposite experiences—same conclusions.

The key, I believe, is that despite differing life stories and distinct cultural traditions, both were dedicated seekers of truth, visionary mystics, and social critics whose deep understanding of people, society, and reality itself led them to express universal truths about being human in the world. As has been said of all the world's major religious traditions, "many paths, one truth."

The Sayings

At certain times, the world begins to make sense. Contradictions melt into meaningful paradoxes, intuitions are corroborated, insights align. Such is the case in this collection of parallel passages from Taoist and Christian scripture, nearly all taken from the mouths of the founders of the traditions themselves, Lao Tzu and Jesus. (A couple of passages are from the Old Testament, which Jesus drew from extensively, and a few are from the writings of St. Paul.)

Separated by hundreds of years and belonging to totally independent cultural traditions, the teachings of Jesus and Lao Tzu show a remarkable kinship. Their sentiments echo one another with a resonance that vibrates through the ages. Sometimes they even use strikingly similar images. Often their words stand as subtle commentaries to one another, a sort of "Tao of Jesus" or "Gospel according to Lao Tzu." How can this be?

When we see deeply into the fabric of reality and begin to grasp the mystery of being alive, the fragmented confusion of human experience dissipates. Cultural barriers fall and one can sense a resonant presence beyond the chaos of being in the world. What is important comes to the fore, effortlessly, and what is trivial is exposed and fades away. Truths become whole instead of partial, and we feel connected to them. Our gaze becomes fixed on what unites rather than divides; we glimpse the unity behind the diversity.

Although they grew out of very different cultures and spiritual traditions, the words of Jesus and Lao Tzu echo one another on a number of topics. Both sages held a vision of an unnameable, ultimate source that dwells in the inmost depths of the individual as well as ruling the heavens. And that vision inspired the way they felt people should conduct their lives. Both extolled the core virtues of humility, gentleness, and integrity while condemning materialism, wealth, injustice, social privilege, hypocrisy, and violence.

This is not to say there aren't significant differences between the two traditions and their founding sages. For one thing, in the Taoist conception, the absolute—the Tao—is an impersonal force that animates the universe, while in the Christian tradition God is usually viewed in a more personal light.

When we examine the contrasts closely, though, we find mostly a difference of emphasis. For example, Taoism essentially is rooted in the natural world, taking the workings of nature as its guide and model, while Christianity adopts a more ambivalent attitude, sometimes reveling in the beauty of the natural world while other times distrusting it and exhibiting a strong world-denying streak. Similarly, Taoism assumes a fundamentally positive view of human nature, at least in its uncorrupted state, while Christianity tends to look at the world and human nature as the aftermath of (i.e., punishment for) a betrayed trust (The Fall), correctible by Christ's intervention. Although we're made in the image of God, we still must cry out for redemption from our fallen state and the burden of original sin.

Also, Christianity in general puts a greater emphasis on immortality and the next world, while Taoism, at least of the philosophical variety, kept its gaze primarily focused on this world. But this too is really only a question of emphasis, considering that Taoism generated a rich tradition of pursuing immortality both in this world and beyond. Indeed, the Taoist pantheon of immortals and spiritual beings is reminiscent of the Christian retinue of saints and angels.

Allowing for such differences, there are intriguing correspondences between the two spiritual traditions. One involves a threefold model of the divine. The Trinity, of course, lies at the heart of the Christian mystery. Yet trinitarian thought is also very important in Taoism. In popular Taoism a trinity of three gods evolved, the Three Pure Ones. The first is Ling Pao (Heaven's Marvelously Responsive Jewel), the embodiment of yin and yang, the masculine and feminine polarities that balance the universe; the second is Yu Luang (The Jade Emperor), embodiment of the forces that set the universe in motion; and the third is Lao Tzu, the author of the Tao Te Ching, embodying Taoist doctrine. Together the three stand for the basic divisions of reality, just as we commonly carve up temporal reality into past, present, and future, or spatial reality into above, below, and here.

But the fundamental Taoist trinity is the Tao of heaven, the Tao of earth, and the Tao of man. The Tao of heaven is clearly the metaphysical Tao, the cosmic absolute that can't be named or grasped, only intuited. The Tao Te Ching states in Chapter 25, "Before Heaven and Earth existed, there was something nebulous, silent, isolated, standing alone, unchanging, eternally revolving, worthy to be called the mother of all things." Chapter 14 describes the metaphysical Tao in this way:

Looked at, but cannot be seen—
that is called the invisible (*yi*).
Listened to, but cannot be heard—
that is called the inaudible (*hsi*).
Grasped at, but cannot be touched—
that is called the intangible (*wei*).
These three elude all our inquiries
and hence blend and become one . . .
That is why it is called the form of the formless,
the image of nothingness.

Clearly this is an attempt to describe the indescribable, the ultimate source of the universe. Despite its unique Chinese expression, the metaphysical Tao is clearly analogous to God the Father in the Christian tradition—the remote source of creation.

The Tao of earth represents Tao manifested in the world (sometimes called *teh*, "virtue," "character" or "power"), the way of the universe and its workings in nature. The orbits of the planets, the cycles of the seasons, the interaction of growth and decay, and so on, all represent this accessible aspect of Tao. But though matter is infused with Tao, the guiding principle ordering all nature is still spirit.

On this level Tao can be thought of as the laws of physics, or in more humanistic terms, natural law. It is impersonal but ultimately benevolent, sustaining and transforming all living things.

The third aspect of the Taoist hierarchy is the Tao of man, or the way humanity's social order ought to be organized. This is the Taoist way applied to human society, a society in accord with the ways of nature, not hostile to it. The Tao Te Ching and the writings of Lao Tzu's great disciple, Chaung Tzu, give innumerable examples of how human society has gone awry by being out of touch with Tao, and how to restore the original balance, putting an end to corruption and depravity. In this respect many of the teachings of Lao Tzu call to mind those of Jesus, often in almost identical language, challenging the structure and practices of an unjust social and economic system that made a mockery of its ancient spiritual ideals. The Tao of man as conceived by Lao Tzu corresponds to the Son of the Christian Trinity, the incarnation of the cosmic spirit into human life.

Jesus and Lao Tzu were essentially teachers, enlightened sages trying to convey their visions to humanity. Like the parables of Jesus, much of the Tao Te Ching is spiritual instruction seeking to show people how they should live and act in accordance with the will of ultimate reality. That being done, it would reform and transform society.

While the source of their teachings may have been mystical and remote, the subject was often closer to home. Both Lao Tzu and Jesus were social commentators. Jesus comes across as more socially engaged and confrontational than the reclusive Lao Tzu, but their critiques were quite similar. Jesus, heir of the prophetic Hebrew tradition, was often more emotional than the mild-tempered Lao Tzu, but they both gave much political and social advice, without compromising their spiritual orientation. Though Jesus provoked the authorities by his quest for social justice (which ultimately cost him his life), he proclaimed that his kingdom was not of this world, thoroughly rejecting an overtly political agenda for his mission.

Despite his passion for social justice and all the turbulence it aroused, Jesus often exhibited the life-engaging sensitivity that we see so prevalent in the gentle Lao Tzu. Indeed, if Jesus had lived to a ripe old age, he might have mellowed like the sage we call Lao Tzu, "the Old Boy." Perhaps that lighter side of Jesus' nature, the part that felt comfortable in the world and delighted in the beauty of nature and the innocence and simplicity of children, would have ripened to fullness with the gift of years.

Over the years, my personal explorations of the Christian and Taoist traditions have led me to perceive the bonds that connect them, despite their deep doctrinal and cultural differences. When their essential messages align, one can see the foundation of what Aldous Huxley called the Perennial Wisdom.

I came to both Christianity and Taoism with an outsider's un-jaundiced point of view, seeking knowledge and wisdom beyond what I had found in the Jewish tradition I grew up in. During the course of that seeking, in the nurturing silence of many hours of study, I felt a particular affinity between the teachings of these two traditions take root in my mind and heart. As I pored over the Gospels and read the Tao Te Ching innumerable times, an organic unity between them seeped into my soul. And it only deepened as I adopted spiritual practices from both: Taoist meditation, Tai Chi, and shiatsu message I engaged in with my Taoist pursuits, and Christian practices of daily prayer, study, and chanting. I also saw the two sages' teachings as profound antidotes to the excesses and afflictions of our culture and modern industrial civilization in general.

This bond was the genesis of this book, as several years ago I began to compile a number of complementary passages from Jesus and Lao Tzu, which I then showed to a Taoist priest. He was intrigued and enthusiastic about the compatibility of the Taoist and Christian wisdom I had collected, but urged me to write commentaries on them. I was reluctant at first to do so because I felt the sages' words stood as commentaries to each other, and I didn't want to impose my particular interpretation on them. But I did write them, and it proved to be a rewarding literary as well as spiritual exercise. My intention in presenting this collection is to give a similar opportunity for readers to discover their own sense of connectedness between the teaching of Jesus and Lao Tzu. I offer my accompanying commentaries (in the back of the book) as a humble aid in that endeavor.

I hope that reflecting on the words of these two remarkable teachers will lead you toward an experience of wholeness, and perhaps leave you with the haunted feeling of having been witness to the oneness of truth.

Martin Aronson
San Francisco, 2000

JESUS AND LAO TZU

The Parallel Sayings

Simplicity

The topic of simplicity is integral to the messages of both Lao Tzu and Jesus. Both sages deeply mistrusted the learned elites of their times—the Confucian mandarins and the Pharisees, respectively— who engineered complex institutions and conventions to control society.

Lao Tzu and Jesus vilified people who used their intellectual talents for exploitation and social advantage, and in contrast extolled the pure of heart and simple of soul. Jesus condemned the learned men of his time as "blind guides," and both he and Lao Tzu instead praised the innocence of a child's unspoiled nature as a far better model to emulate. Both masters enumerated the rewards of pursuing a quiet life of inner contemplation—drawing on the ineffable Source that gives lasting joy and spiritual sustenance. They also both advocated a life of peace and wholeness in which people would enjoy the simple pleasures and virtues of living harmoniously with each other.

Look at the birds of the air; they neither sow nor reap nor gather into barns, and yet your heavenly Father feeds them.

MATTHEW 6:26

L a o   T z u

By doing nothing, everything is done.

Tao Te Ching 48

Martha, Martha, you are busy and bothered about many things; there is need of only one thing. Mary has chosen the better part, which shall not be taken from her.

If you keep your mouth shut
and guard the senses
life is free of toil.
Open your mouth
always be busy
and life is beyond hope.

TAO TE CHING 52

Go into your room and shut the door and pray to your
Father who is in secret; and your Father who sees in secret
will reward you.

MATTHEW 6:5

Without stepping outside
you can know what is happening in the world.
Without looking out the window
you can see the way of heaven.

TAO TE CHING 47

Unless you change and become like children, you will never enter the kingdom of heaven.

MATTHEW 18:3

Being the stream of the universe,
ever true and unswerving,
become as a little child once more.

TAO TE CHING 28

Blessed are the pure of heart, for they will see God.

MATTHEW 5:8

Reveal your simple self,
embrace your original nature.

TAO TE CHING 19

Woe to you lawyers! For you have taken away the key of knowledge; you did not enter yourselves, and you hindered those who were entering.

LUKE 11:52

The wise one does not know many things;
one who knows many things is not wise.

TAO TE CHING 81

At that same hour Jesus rejoiced in the Holy Spirit and said, "I thank you, Father, Lord of heaven and earth, because you have hidden these things from the learned and the intelligent and have revealed them to infants."

LUKE 10:21

Banish "wisdom" and discard "knowledge"
and people will be a hundred times happier.
Banish "kindness" and discard "justice"
and people will remember love for each other.

<small>TAO TE CHING 19</small>

Jesus

Your Father knows what you need before you ask him.

MATTHEW 6:8

The Tao of heaven does not ask,
yet is supplied with all its needs.

TAO TE CHING 73

Why do you call me good? No one is good but God alone.

MARK 10:18

All can see beauty as beauty only because there is ugliness.
All can know good as good only because there is evil.

TAO TE CHING 2

Seek first the kingdom of God and his righteousness, and all things will be given to you.

MATTHEW 6:33

Be really whole
and all things will come to you.

TAO TE CHING 22

Go your way; behold, I send you out as lambs in the midst of wolves. Carry no purse, no sandals, and salute no one on the road. Whatever house you enter, first say, "Peace be to this house!"

LUKE 10:3–5

There is nothing softer or more yielding than water
but none is superior to it in overcoming the hard;
it has no equal.
Weakness overcomes strength
and gentleness overcomes rigidity.
Everyone knows this,
yet no one puts it into practice.

TAO TE CHING 78

A sower went out to sow his seed; and as he sowed, some fell on the path and was trampled on, and the birds of the air ate it up. Some fell on the rock; and as it grew up, it withered for lack of moisture. Some fell among thorns, and the thorns grew with it and choked it. Some fell into good soil, and when it grew, it produced a hundredfold. . . . Let anyone with ears to hear listen!

LUKE 8:5–8

When the wisest people hear of the Tao
they try hard to live in accordance with it.
When average people hear of the Tao
they give it thought now and again.
When foolish people hear of the Tao
they break into laughter.
If they didn't laugh, it wouldn't be the Tao.

TAO TE CHING 41

Jesus

Ask, and it will be given you; search, and you will find;
knock, and the door will be opened for you.

The spirit of the valley never dies.

It is called the mystic female.

Her door is the root of heaven and earth.

Continuously,

it seems to remain.

Draw upon it

and it serves you with ease.

TAO TE CHING 6

Blessed are the poor in spirit,

for theirs is the kingdom of heaven.

Blessed are those who mourn, for they will be comforted.

Blessed are the meek, for they will inherit the earth.

Blessed are those who hunger and thirst for righteousness,

for they will be filled.

Blessed are the merciful, for they will receive mercy.

Blessed are the pure in heart, for they will see God.

Blessed are the peacemakers,

for they will be called children of God.

MATTHEW 5:3–9

To yield is to be preserved whole.
To be bent is to become straight.
To be hollow is to be filled.
To be tattered is to be renewed.
To be in want is to possess.
To have plenty is to be confused.

TAO TE CHING 22

But woe to you who are rich,

for you have received your consolation.

Woe to you who are full now,

for you will be hungry.

Woe to you who are laughing now,

for you will mourn and weep.

LUKE 6:24–25

That which shrinks
must first expand.
That which becomes weak
must first be strong.
That which is cast down
must first be raised.
Those who are taken away from
must first be given.

TAO TE CHING 36

And can any of you by worrying add a single hour to the span of your life?

LUKE 12:25

The Tao of heaven does not strive,
and yet it overcomes.

Materialism

Lao Tzu and Jesus were unfailing opponents of the passion for wealth and the preoccupation with material things. They saw clearly the negative, stunting effects of materialism on human lives and repudiated it as a sort of disease.

Materialistic concerns, almost by definition, are a spiritual danger because they impede the deepening and leavening necessary for cultivating an inner life. To Lao Tzu wealth, more than anything else, was a burden—a source of anxiety and a time-consuming diversion from far more important matters. "When gold and jade fill your hall, you will not be able to keep them safe," he flatly declares. To Jesus, wealth was a pernicious distraction. "What does it profit a man if he gains the whole world and loses his soul?" he pointedly asks. Both saw wealth for the delusion it is and condemned it vociferously. But they both also knew what real treasure is—the treasure of a good heart.

Do not worry about your life, what you will eat, or about your body, what you will wear. For life is more than food, and the body more than clothing.

LUKE 12:22

The sage does not accumulate things.
He lives for other people
and grows richer himself.
He gives to other people
and has greater abundance.

TAO TE CHING 81

What does it profit them if they gain the whole world,
but lose their souls?

To be proud with wealth and honor
is to sow the seeds of your own downfall.

Tao Te Ching 9

Take care! Be on your guard against all kinds of greed; for one's life does not consist in the abundance of his possessions.

Luke 12:15

There is no greater curse than discontentment,
No greater sin than the desire for possession.

TAO TE CHING 46

Store up for yourselves treasures in heaven.

MATTHEW 6:20

Lao Tzu

I have three treasures—guard them, keep them safe.
The first is love
the second is moderation
the third is daring not to be ahead of others.

TAO TE CHING 67

For where your treasure is, there your heart will be also.

MATTHEW 6:21

The sage wears rough clothing
and holds the jewel in his heart.

TAO TE CHING 70

"No servant can serve two masters; for either he will hate the one and love the other, or be devoted to the one and despise the other. You cannot serve God and wealth." The Pharisees, who were lovers of money, heard all this, and they scoffed at him. So he said to them, "You are those who justify yourselves in the sight of others, but God knows your hearts; for what is prized by human beings is an abomination in the sight of God."

LUKE 16:13−15

The Tao of heaven is to take from those who have too
much and give to those who do not have enough.
Man's way is different.
He takes from those who do not have enough
and gives to those who already have too much.
What man has more than enough
and gives it to the world?
Only the man of Tao.

TAO TE CHING 77

Do not store up for yourselves treasures on earth, where moth and rust consume and where thieves break in and steal.

MATTHEW 6:19

When gold and jade fill your hall,
you will not be able to keep them safe.

T<small>AO</small> T<small>E</small> C<small>HING</small> 77

Humility

Humility is a prime virtue for both Lao Tzu and Jesus—one could almost call it the mother virtue from which all the others spring. A humble heart, purged of conceit and selfishness, is the mark of a gentle and admirable character.

Lao Tzu continually warned against the dangers of striving for rank and position and repeatedly admonished that the sage "does not pride himself and is therefore chief among men." Jesus similarly maintained that "the first will be last and the last first." He loved and encouraged the poor and humble of station, and embodied the virtue of humility in many aspects of his life, particularly in his healing work.

Jesus

The least among all of you is the greatest.

LUKE 9:48

4

The best of people is like water.
Water gives life to all things
and does not compete with them.
It flows in places people reject
and so is like the Tao.

All who exalt themselves will be humbled,
and all who humble themselves will be exalted.

Matthew 23:12

The sage puts himself last
and finds himself in the foremost place.

TAO TE CHING 7

The Son of Man came not to be served but to serve.

MATTHEW 20:28

If the sage would guide the people,

he must serve with humility.

If he would lead them, he must follow behind.

In this way when the sage rules,

the people will not feel oppressed;

when he stands before them, they will not be harmed.

Because he does not contend

no one can contend against him.

TAO TE CHING 66

Blessed are the meek, for they will inherit the earth.

MATTHEW 5:5

Heaven arms with gentleness
those it would not see destroyed.

Once, when Jesus was in one of the cities, there was a man covered with leprosy. When he saw Jesus, he bowed with his face to the ground and begged him, "Lord, if you choose, you can make me clean." Then Jesus stretched out his hand, touched him, and said, "I do choose. Be made clean." Immediately the leprosy left him. And he ordered him to tell no one. "Go," he said, "and show yourself to the priest, and, as Moses commanded, make an offering for your cleansing, for a testimony to them." But now more than ever the word about Jesus spread abroad; many crowds would gather to hear him and to be cured of their diseases. But he would withdraw to deserted places and pray.

LUKE 5:12–16

Those who are familiar with honor and glory
but keep to obscurity
become the valley of the world.
Being the valley of the world,
they have an eternal power that always suffices.

Tao Te Ching 28

Many that are first will be last, and the last will be first.

MARK 10:31

Softness and gentleness are the companions of life.

The hard and strong will fall.

The soft and weak will overcome.

TAO TE CHING 76

Many crowds followed him, and he cured all of them,
and he ordered them not to make him known.

MATTHEW 12:16

The wise embrace the one
and set an example to all.
Not putting on a display,
they shine forth.
Not justifying themselves,
they are distinguished.
Not boasting,
they receive recognition.

TAO TE CHING 22

Those who speak on their own seek their own glory; but the one who seeks the glory of him who sent him is true, and there is nothing false in him.

Those who know do not talk.
Those who talk do not know.

TAO TE CHING 56

When the wine gave out, the mother of Jesus said to him,
"They have no wine." And Jesus said to her, "Woman,
what concern is that to you and to me? My hour has not
yet come."

John 2:3–4

Through not presuming to be first in the world
one can develop one's talent and let it mature.

TAO TE CHING 67

Love

In all its varied forms and wondrous manifestations, love is the raison d'etre of human life, the most powerful force we encounter in ourselves. Jesus and Lao Tzu recognized this and sought to transform peoples' hearts and remake society by means of this awesome force.

Both teachers warned against responding with harsh judgment against those whose actions we disapprove of. Jesus implored us to even "Love our enemies, do good to those who hate you," and Lao Tzu advised us to "Requite hatred with virtue." This was surely their most demanding challenge. But they also instructed us to sometimes be neutral or nonjudgmental when encountering what is evil or unjust, imitating the model of God or nature in its restraint and detachment. Indeed, Lao Tzu and Jesus urged us to trust in the ultimate power to set things right in due course.

Sometimes the type of love they exhorted us to demonstrate is easier and more down to earth—forgiving a truly contrite person, exercising tolerance, or displaying simple kindness and tenderness. In any case, they did not view love and forgiveness as idealistic fantasies or impractical luxuries, but as the primary tools for changing the world.

Love your neighbor as yourself.

MATTHEW 22:39

Love the world as your own self.

TAO TE CHING 13

Love is patient; love is kind; love is not envious or boastful
or arrogant or rude. It does not insist on its own way; it is
not irritable or resentful; it does not rejoice in wrong-
doing, but rejoices in the truth. It bears all things, believes
all things, hopes all things, endures all things.

I Corinthians 13:4–7

Love is victorious in attack
and invulnerable in defense.

TAO TE CHING 67

A lawyer asked him a question, "Teacher, which commandment in the law is the greatest?" He said to him, "'You shall love the Lord your God with all your heart, and with all your soul, and with all your mind.' This is the greatest and first commandment. And a second is like it: 'You shall love your neighbor as yourself.' On these two commandments hang all the law and the prophets."

MATTHEW 22:35–40

To return to the root is repose.

Going back to one's destiny is to find the eternal law.

To know the eternal law is enlightenment.

TAO TE CHING 16

Be children of your Father in heaven; for he makes his sun rise on the evil and on the good, and sends rain on the righteous and on the unrighteous.

MATTHEW 5:45

Heaven and earth join
and sweet rain falls
beyond the command of people
yet evenly upon all.

TAO TE CHING 32

Do not judge, and you will not be judged; do not condemn, and you will not be condemned. Forgive, and you will be forgiven.

LUKE 6:37

The sage is good to people who are good.

He is also good to people who aren't good.

This is true goodness.

The sage trusts people who are trustworthy.

He also trusts people who aren't trustworthy.

This is true trust.

Tao Te Ching 49

Let anyone among you who is without sin be the first to throw a stone.

JOHN 8:7

We can seize and kill the unruly,
but who would dare to do so?
Often it happens that the executioner is killed.
He who takes the hatchet of the master carpenter
seldom escapes injury to his own hands.

TAO TE CHING 74

Do not resist an evildoer. If anyone strikes you on the right cheek, offer him the other also.

MATTHEW 5:38

Respond to anger with virtue.

TAO TE CHING 63

Jesus

The Son of Man came to save, not condemn.

MATTHEW 18:11

People may not be good, but do not reject them.

TAO TE CHING 62

Love your enemies, do good to those who hate you.

LUKE 6:27

The sage is good at helping everyone.
For that reason there is no rejected person.
Therefore the good man is the teacher of the bad
and the bad man is the lesson of the good.

TAO TE CHING 27

Take heed to yourselves; if your brother sins, rebuke him; and if he repents, forgive him; and if he sins against you seven times in the day, and turns to you seven times, and says, "I repent," you must forgive him.

LUKE 17:3–4

The way of Heaven is impartial;
it sides only with the good person.

Little children, I am with you only a little longer. I give you a new commandment, that you love one another. Just as I have loved you, you also should love one another.

John 13:33–34

When the sage lives with people,
they live harmoniously together.
The sage regards them all as his own children.

TAO TE CHING 49

Hypocrisy

Naturally enough, Jesus' and Lao Tzu's disdain for the evil of hypocrisy grew out of their love for the virtues of simplicity and innocence. For those who remain simple in spirit rarely engage in hypocrisy, and those who retain their natural innocence usually abhor violence.

Hypocrisy encompasses a wide swath of society's ills. It's the primary vehicle used by social elites to perpetuate their dominance and ensure positions of privilege. The Pharisees and priests in Jesus' case, and the Confucian ministers in Lao Tzu's case, became the architects of corrupt, unjust, and spiritually bankrupt societies, constructed at the expense of those they ruled. No other subject elicits such deep indignation on the part of Jesus and Lao Tzu, and both sages unleash their most vehement language to attack and condemn it. Lao Tzu accuses the courtiers of "splitting with wealth and possession" and "leading the world toward brigandage." Jesus rails at the Pharisees, saying they "seem outwardly upright . . . but inside are full of extortion and rapacity."

Woe to you, scribes and Pharisees, hypocrites! For you are like whitewashed tombs, which on the outside look beautiful, but inside they are full of the bones of the dead and of all kinds of filth. So you also on the outside look righteous to others, but inside you are full of hypocrisy and lawlessness.

MATTHEW 23:27–28

He who boasts achieves nothing.

He who takes pride in himself is not chief among people.

According to followers of the Tao,

These are the "dregs and tumors of virtue,"

things of disgust.

Therefore followers of the Tao spurn them.

TAO TE CHING 24

Then the Pharisees went and plotted to entrap him in what he said, saying, "Teacher, we know that you are sincere, and teach the way of God in accordance with truth, and show deference to no one; for you do not regard people with partiality. Tell us, then, what you think. Is it lawful to pay taxes to the emperor, or not?" But Jesus, aware of their malice, said, "Why are you putting me to the test, you hypocrites?"

MATTHEW 22:15–18

He who neither values his teacher
nor loves the lesson
is one gone far astray
though he be learned.

TAO TE CHING 27

Isaiah prophesied rightly about you hypocrites, as it is
written,

    This people honors me with their lips,

    but their hearts are far from me;

    in vain do they worship me,

    teaching human precepts as doctrines.

You abandon the commandment of God and hold to the
tradition of men.

MARK 7:6

Ritual is the husk of faith and loyalty,
the beginning of confusion.

Tao Te Ching 38

Alas for you scribes and Pharisees, hypocrites, for as
pretext for your piety you pray long prayers, yet cheat
widows out of their houses.

MATTHEW 23:14

Lao Tzu

On the decline of the great Tao
the doctrines of "humanity" and "morality" arose.
When knowledge and cleverness appeared,
great hypocrisy followed in its wake.

TAO TE CHING 18

Beware of the yeast of the Pharisees, that is, their hypocrisy.

Luke 12:1

When there is strife in the family,
people talk about "brotherly love."
When the country falls into chaos,
politicians talk about "patriotism."

TAO TE CHING 18

The scribes and the Pharisees sit on Moses' seat; so
practice and observe what they tell you, but not what they
do; for they do not practice what they teach. They tie up
heavy burdens, hard to bear, and lay them on the
shoulders of others . . . they love the place of honor at
feasts and the best seats in the synagogue, and salutations
in the market places. . . . Woe to you, scribes and
Pharisees, hypocrites! for you tithe mint and dill and
cumin, and have neglected the weightier matters of the
law: justice, mercy and faith. . . . On the outside you
look righteous to others, but inside you are full of
extortion and rapacity.

MARK 10:23–25

When the court is arrayed in splendor
the fields are full of weeds
and the granaries are bare.
Some wear gorgeous clothes,
carry fine swords,
and indulge themselves with food and drink;
they are splitting with wealth and possessions.
They are robber barons.
This is certainly the corruption of Tao.

TAO TE CHING 53

Violence

Regarding violence—a deadly form of hypocrisy—both Jesus and Lao Tzu wearily denounce it as humankind's most regrettable vice. Force is not the way of Tao, admonishes Lao Tzu, and "he who is against Tao perishes young."

And Jesus, when witness to violence in his own defense, simply says, "No more of this," and puts a stop to it.

Both sages categorically reject all manner of violence—the psychological violence of social oppression as well as the physical brutality that wreaks so much harm in its path.

When those who were around him saw what was coming, they asked, "Lord, should we strike with the sword?" Then one of them struck the slave of the high priest and cut off his right ear. But Jesus said, "No more of this!" And he touched his ear and healed him.

LUKE 22:49–51

Whoever by Tao resolves to help the ruler
will oppose all conquest by force of arms.

TAO TE CHING 30

You know that the rulers of the Gentiles lord it over them, and their great ones are tyrants over them. It will not be so among you.

MATTHEW 20:25

When a man of authority acts and no one responds,
he rolls up his sleeves to force it on others.

The seventy disciples returned with joy, saying, "Lord, in your name even the demons submit to us!" He said to them, "I watched Satan fall from heaven like a flash of lightning. See, I have given you authority to tread on snakes and scorpions, and over all the power of the enemy; and nothing will hurt you. Nevertheless, do not rejoice at this, that the spirits submit to you, but rejoice that your names are written in heaven."

LUKE 10:17–20

Victory is no cause for rejoicing.
If you rejoice in victory, then you delight in slaughter;
If you delight in slaughter you will not succeed
in your ambition to rule the world.
Enter the battle gravely
with hearts full of sorrow.
A victory must be observed like a funeral.

TAO TE CHING 31

Blessed are the peacemakers, for they will be called children of God.

MATTHEW 5:9

Force is followed by loss of strength.

This is not the way of Tao.

And that which goes against Tao perishes young.

TAO TE CHING 30

All who take the sword will perish by the sword.

MATTHEW 26:52

A violent man will die a violent death.

Wisdom

In the pronouncements of Jesus and Lao Tzu you can hear the penetrating ring of truth reverberate like a resonant bell. "All things are possible with God," declares Jesus. "He who has not enough faith will not be able to command it from others," asserts Lao Tzu.

Lao Tzu and Jesus offered a way to follow in the world to get the deepest meaning and greatest value from it; they also pointed out how to transcend the world. Sometimes treading these paths can be arduous. The journey can be lonely and frustrating, as evidenced occasionally by both Jesus and Lao Tzu expressing that they feel out of place in this world and exasperated with humanity's shortcomings. But more often the path is full of the promise of deliverance and perfect happiness in the embrace of the Absolute.

Be perfect, as your heavenly Father is perfect.

MATTHEW 5:48

Man models himself after the earth.

The earth models itself after heaven.

Heaven models itself after Tao.

Tao models itself after what is natural.

TAO TE CHING 25

You will know them by their fruits.

MATTHEW 7:16

L a o   T z u

Knowing the mother, one also knows the sons.

TAO TE CHING 52

For now we see through a glass darkly, but then we will see face to face. Now I know only in part; then I will know fully, even as I have been fully known.

I Corinthians 13:12

Some things are not favored by heaven. Who knows why?
Even the sage is unsure of this.

Do not think that I have come to bring peace on earth; I have not come to bring peace, but a sword. For I have come to set a man against his father, and a daughter against her mother.

MATTHEW 10:34–35

Nature is not kind.

It treats the creation like sacrificial straw dogs.

The sage is not kind.

He treats people like sacrificial straw dogs.

TAO TE CHING 5

There was in the synagogue a man who had a demon, and he cried out, "What have you to do with us, Jesus of Nazareth? Have you come to destroy us? I know who you are, the Holy one of God." But Jesus rebuked him, saying, "Be silent, and come out of him!" And the demon, convulsing him and crying with a loud voice, came out of him, having done him no harm.

MARK 1:23–26

Approach the universe with Tao
and evil will have no power.
Not that evil is not powerful—
but its power will not be used to harm others.

TAO TE CHING 60

Why are you afraid, you of little faith?

MATTHEW 8:26

He who has not enough faith
will not be able to command faith from others.

TAO TE CHING 23

Jesus

He who rules his spirit has won a greater victory than the taking of a city.

PROVERBS 16:32

He who knows others is learned;
he who knows himself is wise
He who conquers others has power of muscles;
he who conquers himself is strong.

Tao Te Ching 33

Now Jesus stood before the governor; and the governor asked him, "Are you the King of the Jews?" Jesus said, "You say so." But when he was accused by the chief priests and elders, he did not answer. Then Pilate said to him, "Do you not hear how many accusations they make against you?" But he gave him no answer, not even to a single charge, so that the governor was greatly amazed.

MATTHEW 27:11–14

The softest thing in the universe
overcomes the hardest.
Something that has no substance
penetrates even where there is no space.
This teaches me the value of non-action.
Teaching without words and work without doing
are understood by very few.

TAO TE CHING 43

Come to me, all you that are weary and carrying heavy
burdens, and I will give you rest. Take my yoke upon you,
and learn from me; for I am gentle and humble in heart,
and you will find rest for your souls. For my yoke is easy,
and my burden is light.

MATTHEW 11:28–30

All people will come to the person
who keeps to the One,
for there lie rest and happiness and peace.

Thomas said to him, "Lord, we do not know where you are going. How can we know the way?" Jesus said to him, "I am the way, and the truth, and the life."

JOHN 14:5–6

If I have even just a little sense,
I will walk on the main road and my only fear
will be of straying from it.
Keeping to the main road is easy,
but people love to be sidetracked.

TAO TE CHING 53

Foxes have holes and birds have nests, but the Son of Man has nowhere to lay his head.

Luke 9:58

The people are contented, enjoying sacrificial feasts.
In spring some go to the park and climb the terrace,
but I alone am drifting, not knowing where I am.
Like a newborn babe before it learns to smile,
I am alone, without a home.

TAO TE CHING 20

With God all things are possible.

MATTHEW 19:26

If there is a good store of virtue,
then nothing is impossible.

TAO TE CHING 59

Whoever would save his life will lose it, and whoever loses his life for my sake will save it.

The sage regards his body as accidental
and his body is thereby preserved.

TAO TE CHING 7

He who endures to the end will be saved.

John 14:27

A journey of a thousand miles starts under one's feet.

Tao Te Ching 64

Mysticism

Jesus and Lao Tzu, above all else, were mystics, concerned with seeing into and experiencing the ultimate nature of reality. This is the foundation on which their philosophical and social message rests. Their prime teaching was to understand and identify with the source from which all being flows, and then to pattern one's life in accord with it.

They give us numerous examples of their attempts to express the inexpressible. Lao Tzu talks of the Tao as "something nebulous, silent, isolated, unchanging," or "an image of what existed before God." Jesus spoke of God the Father and offered several nature metaphors of the kingdom of heaven to convey an inkling of the mystery of God's being. Connecting to the animating principle of the universe—the Tao of heaven manifesting in the world, or God both before and after Creation—was the essence of their vision.

In the beginning was the Word, and the Word was with God, and the Word was God.

JOHN I:I

Before heaven and earth existed
there was something nebulous:
silent, isolated
standing alone, not changing,
eternally revolving without fail,
worthy to be the mother of all things.
I do not know its name.
I address it as Tao.
If forced to give it a name,
I shall call it "Great."

TAO TE CHING 25

Truly, truly I say to you, the Son can do nothing of his own accord, but only what he sees the Father doing. . . . For as the Father raises the dead and gives them life, so also the Son gives life to whom he will. The Father judges no one, but has given all judgment to the Son, that all may honor the Son, even as they honor the Father.

John 5:19–23

Tao gives them birth
Teh fosters them.
Therefore all things of the universe
worship Tao and exalt *Teh*.
Tao is worshiped and *Teh* exalted
without anyone's order but
of its own accord.

TAO TE CHING 5I

Jesus

Know and understand that the Father is in me and I am in the Father; I and the Father are one.

The nameless is the origin of heaven and earth;
the named is the mother of all things.
These two are the same;
they are only given different names
when they become manifest.
They both may be called the cosmic mystery.

TAO TE CHING I

Consider the lilies of the field, how they grow; they neither toil nor spin, yet I tell you, even Solomon in all his glory was not clothed like one of these.

MATTHEW 6:28–29

From the days of old till now
Its named, manifested forms have never ceased,
By which we may view the father of all things
How do I know the shape of the father of all things?
Through these things of the created world!

TAO TE CHING 21

Heaven and earth will pass away, but my words will not pass away.

Luke 21:33

The ten thousand things rise and fall
but the way of nature is unchanging.
Being at one with the Tao is eternal.
And though the body passes away,
the Tao will never pass away.

TAO TE CHING 16

One day he got into a boat with his disciples, and he said to them, "Let us go across to the other side of the lake." So they set out, and while they were sailing he fell asleep. A windstorm swept down on the lake, and the boat was filling with water, and they were in danger. They went to him and woke him up, shouting, "Master, Master, we are perishing!" And he woke up and rebuked the wind and the raging waves; they ceased, and there was a calm. He said to them, "Where is your faith?" They were afraid and amazed, and said to one another, "Who then is this, that he commands even the winds and the water, and they obey him?"

LUKE 8:22–25

Who is calm and quiet becomes
the guide for the universe.

The kingdom of heaven is like a mustard seed that someone took and sowed in his field; it is the smallest of all the seeds, but when it has grown it is the greatest of shrubs and becomes a tree, so that the birds of the air come and make nests in its branches.

MATTHEW 13:31–32

The Tao is forever undefined.

Small though it is, it cannot be grasped.

Tao in the world is like a river flowing home to the sea.

TAO TE CHING 32

For everything there is a season, and a time for every purpose under heaven.

ECCLESIASTES 3:1

All things take shape and rise to activity
but I watch them fall back to rest,
like vegetation that grows luxuriantly
and returns to the soil it springs from.

TAO TE CHING 16

As he walked by the Sea of Galilee, he saw two brothers, Simon who is called Peter and Andrew his brother, casting a net into the sea; for they were fishermen. And he said to them, "Follow me, and I will make you fishers of men."

MATTHEW 4:18–19

Heaven's net covers the whole universe.
Though its meshes are wide, nothing slips through.

TAO TE CHING 73

The kingdom of God is among you.

LUKE 17:21

The great Tao flows everywhere.

TAO TE CHING 34

Immortality

In one way or another, no one is untouched by tragedy—it is part of the human condition. This reality led the Buddha to conclude that "existence" is suffering, that there is something fundamentally out of joint in our world and that life itself is a problem to be solved. Jesus was acutely aware of evil, and many times expressed his disdain for the world and its ways. Even the generally life-affirming Lao Tzu acknowledged the world's tendency to wallow in ignorance and vileness, and lamented that the way of gentleness and natural goodness is commonly scorned, if not outright punished.

One thing tragedies remind us of is to not inflict pain and suffering on our own part, if we can help it. The other great lesson of suffering falls on the side of the victim—that is, how we respond to whatever heartbreak life hands us. Sometimes we are asked to accept the unacceptable. But tragedy in our lives can force us to discover resources and strengths we never dreamed we possessed.

Every human being is the melding of spirit and matter, and in a life well lived that union may be a happy one, filled with richness and delight. Jesus and Lao Tzu saw this and refused to grant suffering and physical death the final word on human destiny.

Truly, truly, I say to you, he who believes has eternal life.

JOHN 6:47

He who dies yet his power remains has long life.

TAO TE CHING 33

It is the spirit that gives life; the flesh is useless. The words that I have spoken to you are spirit and life.

JOHN 6:63

Those who know how to live can walk abroad
without fear of rhinoceros or tiger.
They can enter battle without being wounded.
The rhinoceros can find no place to thrust its horn,
the tiger no place to use its claws,
and weapons no place to pierce.
Why is this?
Because they are beyond death.

TAO TE CHING 50

I tell you, my friends, do not fear those who kill the body, and after that can do nothing more. But I will warn you whom to fear: fear him who, after he has killed, has authority to cast into hell.

LUKE 12:4–5

If the people are not afraid of death,
why would they fear threats of death?

TAO TE CHING 74

In the world you will face tribulation. But take courage; I have overcome the world!

JOHN 16:33

Who understands Tao seems uncomprehending.
Who is advanced in Tao seems to slip backwards.
Who moves on the even path
seems to bounce up and down.

TAO TE CHING 41

Not everyone who says to me, "Lord, Lord," will enter the kingdom of heaven, but only the one who does the will of my Father in heaven. On that day many will say to me, "Lord, Lord. . . ." Then I will declare to them, "I never knew you; go away from me."

MATTHEW 7:21−23

My teachings are easy to understand and easy to practice,
yet no one knows them or practices them.
In my words there is a principle.
In human affairs there is a system.
Because people don't know these things
they don't know me either.

Tao Te Ching 70

Enter through the narrow gate; for the gate is wide and the road is easy that leads to destruction, and there are many who take it. For the gate is narrow and the road is hard that leads to life, and there are few who find it.

MATTHEW 7:13–14

Few people understand me.
This is why I am distinguished.

TAO TE CHING 70

He was despised and rejected by others; a man of sorrows
and acquainted with grief; surely he has borne our griefs
and carried our sorrows, yet we accounted him stricken,
struck down by God and afflicted. But he was wounded
for our transgressions; therefore I will allot him a portion
with the great . . . because he poured out his soul to
death, and was numbered with the transgressors, yet bore
the sin of many and made intercession for the
transgressors.

ISAIAH 53:3–12

He who takes upon himself the slander of the world
is the preserver of the state.
He who takes upon himself the sins of the world
is the king of the world.

TAO TE CHING 78

Commentaries

Simplicity

pages 4–5

How often we make a mess of things in our busyness and compulsion! If we trusted more in the benevolence of nature, we could limit our agitation and spasms of destructiveness. There is as much wisdom in knowing when not to do something as there is in knowing when to act. If we become more contemplative and gentle, nature brings itself into harmony and things heal of their own accord, as does a wound if given the chance.

pages 6–7

A calm, peaceful state of mind is the basis of insight and emotional well-being. To lead a hectic, agitated life, continually beset by cares and responsibilities, crowds out the possibility of deeper nourishment.

pages 8–9

Chasing around, seeing and doing many things can be a type of emotional consumerism. Its rewards are fleeting at best, and much of the time venturing out in the world is a stress-filled, vexatious experience. If you can tap into the source of all peace and fullness in your own room, why go out?

pages 10–11

Children, in their innocence, guilelessness, and sensitivity, are the obvious model of the natural integrity needed to grow spiritually. When that innocence is seasoned with the maturity life brings, a higher stage of integrity is realized. We can grow older while transforming our natural innocence into something richer—becoming like a rare wise and gentle child.

pages 12–13

The deepest truths are simple, and the deepest truth of all is character—possessing a pure heart. Truth is resonant, not complex. It reverberates with a direct power, deepening in intensity. A pure heart and a simple self cut through all the static.

pages 14–15

Information is no substitute for wisdom. Lawyers, "scholars," scientists, and businesspeople manipulate information, bending and twisting the truth for their benefit until it is unrecognizable. This is not knowledge—merely its perversion. Real knowledge, wisdom, marries clear thinking with deep feeling.

pages 16–17
By applying only the critical intellect, the lawyers, the scientists, the technicians wrap themselves in a suffocating blanket, misguidedly thinking they can solve all ills by calculation while in fact only cutting themselves off from human feeling and real understanding. Despiritualized learning is the plague of civilization—ancient as well as modern.

pages 18–19
We don't need to plead our case with God, if we approach with a reverent and sincere heart. For God knows our hearts, knows what we need to be good and whole. In our prayers or meditation, we only need to get back to our true selves with genuine intention, and then the good things we need can arise.

pages 20–21
So much of our perception is subject to delusion. We do our best to recognize value, and sometimes, by chance, we hit the mark. But what is really good in the grand scheme of things? We can't know—we simply don't have the necessary information or comprehension. We approximate and judge by means of contrasts, often interpreting things in a short-sighted fashion. Glimpses of truth that transcend human convention and relative thinking are rare.

pages 22–23
When we are attuned to the completeness of the universe, the specifics eventually fall into place—that is, if the world we are a part of is not too far out of balance itself. But even then, there is a power working to right things, and those that are wise can tap into it.

pages 24–25
Jesus charged his disciples with putting into practice Lao Tzu's challenge. A revolutionary way of living—to dare to be gentle in a hostile world and see what fruit may come of it.

pages 26–27

For whatever reasons, people vary in their spiritual sensibilities, a fact that accounts for much of the confusion and lack of communication in the everyday world. This is not a defect of character—rather a difference of temperament and aptitude. But sooner or later, there are lessons that all people must grasp—however long it takes them to flower.

pages 28–29

Cultivating the inner life is the key to understanding reality. Knock on the door within. There the mystery of the world may be revealed, for you are the world in microcosm. The same forces that drive the heavens swirl inside you, and all knowledge of value is accessible within. It is always there, and it will nourish you.

pages 30–31

Christ's beatitudes and the Taoist version echo one another in their grasp of the law of complements. Their sense differs slightly but their proclamation is similar: Things that appear different are very much connected in that they contain elements of their seeming opposites. One only need remain open in awareness to see how things transform into one another, ultimately *are* one another. Nature abhors a void; so all things will be fulfilled. Remaining simple and untainted is the key. All experience seeks balance in its complement, even if the intellect is slow to comprehend in its dullness.

pages 32–33

There is a cyclic drama inherent in every portion of nature—and all points in that drama are mere stages along the way—whether our perspective is broad enough to perceive that vision or not. Reality is dynamic, subject to many forces that drive it on, and always, above all else, it seeks balance. The Greeks called this drama *hubris* and *nemesis*, the Hindus the law of karma. It asserts the same truth—that arrogance, agitation, and domination are not the ultimate way of nature, and they will be leveled in due course.

pages 34–35

Straining and striving, with great anxiousness over some desired outcome, are self-punishing. Patience and faith—taking things in stride while working consistently and constructively—most likely bring about good results. Certainly pointless worrying doesn't help. A simple teaching so easily forgotten in the storm of fear and stress.

Materialism

pages 38–39

Every traditional culture recognizes generosity as the key to a life of abundance. Real wealth is the richness of experience—a sense of organic connectedness to life. Our culture's focus on "things" promotes a tragic waste. Even good, benevolent people are often enmeshed in the delusion of accumulation. How can objects assert such power? Only by our living on the most superficial level. Any deeper experience, whether joyful or tragic, exposes the illusion.

pages 40–41

How can a person build character and be attuned to what is most valuable if absorbed in banalities? Wealth and worldly status fool us into thinking we've fulfilled our task, lessening the likelihood that we even notice what we're missing until our malaise becomes severe. It isn't possible to tread two paths at once—you dwell either in living spirit or fallen matter.

pages 42–43

Seeking gratification by accumulating dead objects indicates a dead soul. Absorption in material things and the status attendant upon them is degrading to the dignity of the soul. Why opt for the vulgar? Awake to the living.

pages 44–45

The treasures of character speak for themselves. They carry a merit in, through, and beyond the natural world.

pages 46–47

The jewel, the treasure, is the quality of one's heart. Keep it innocent, gentle, simple, and wise. What dense metal, heavy fabric, or lifeless stone can compare with that?

pages 48–49

Corrupt society, based on exploitation, reinforces and multiplies all the ignorance, pettiness, and selfishness found in the individual heart. Its conventions, mores, and attitudes will most often be at odds with natural law, God's law. How could society, with its narrow, mean-spirited vision, have any inkling of true justice—the justice that fills rather than takes? Only the person purged of society's lucre and hypocrisy can preserve the higher vision.

pages 50–51

There is no spiritual security in material wealth. At best it can only be a cushion; more often it is either a burden or an outright liability. True security, the quality of character, is not so transitory or crude. Anything alive is infinitely more valuable than anything that is not.

Humility

pages 54–55

The mark of true greatness is humility. To be great is to remain unobtrusive and humble—not to contend for rank or recognition, only to pursue truth. A great soul simply unfolds itself innocuously—helping, nurturing, creating—with no thought of self-aggrandizement, just expression of that virtue.

pages 56–57

Braggadocio and self-promotion don't endure—people lose patience with them. Stripped of pretension, arrogance, artifice, and illusion, a simple and unassuming character is the stamp of a noble nature. The unaffected will eventually rise in esteem, in the eyes of both men and God.

To be puffed up with self-importance is ignorance of the vilest sort. The desire to feel superior usually rests on no healthful basis. In following such a course, one will surely become polluted by selfishness and conceit. To crave status and prestige indicates a shallow, unenlightened character, with little sense as to what is valuable.

Gentleness is the key to eternity, as it is the crown of justice. Inherent in the structure of nature is the reality that all things will be set right, that all promise will be fulfilled, that all goodness will be redeemed. And gentleness is the greatest goodness.

Jesus healed the sick and inspired the poor, but always tried to remain as inconspicuous as possible. He valued acting in the world to ease misery and spread hope, but understood that fame would arouse opposition and endanger his efforts. Without ever having heard of them, he exemplified Lao Tzu's dictates. He tasted honor and glory, yet sought refuge in lonely places to take sustenance from truth. That is where he drew his power from.

Water, the most flexible substance, can nevertheless cut a channel through hard rock. Like water, natural justice seeks its own level. All perversity will be leveled. The energies of the universe are luminous, and will overcome the darker energies of the earth. The cosmic forces turn and reinstate equilibrium in the grand scheme, because justice is intrinsic to them.

There was no self-glorification in Jesus, just healing. He did not promote himself—in fact he took pains to keep himself unknown. But his fame and stature still grew, because any thought of ego had long since been left behind. Lao Tzu would have applauded his method.

Jesus spoke a fair amount, but only as much as necessary. Lao Tzu was similarly sparing with his words, and wrote them out only as a favor to a border guard—thus we know his wisdom. But people who set themselves up as authorities to satisfy their own sense of self-importance are benefitting no one. Even if their motives are in part benevolent, their message is usually muddled.

pages 70–71
One needs a degree of humility for the patience to let one's talent mature. It's not something that should be rushed. Jesus' hidden years are a good example of that. However he spent them—whether studying in India, or more likely working in his father's carpentry shop—they were a time of preparation and unfolding. Striving for prominence and commanding attention before one is ready is foolish. One shouldn't try to fulfill one's destiny until it is ripe.

Love

pages 74–75
You and the world abide in each other. Erase the boundary and let the light flow out and then back in. Diffuse the mystic vision outward, back into the world. An upright heart will enfold the world.

pages 76–77
Love is the final word in the law of nature. All things bow before it, all worldly concerns vanish in its presence. Above and beyond the world is an absolute, unconditional spirit of acceptance, completeness. Some call it divine love. We know it annihilates all.

pages 78–79
If we rest in God, connect to the source of our being, good things will come. Principal among them is love, in all its varied and fulfilling forms. This is the eternal law, the great commandment. Love is the law of the universe. To rest in God or return to Tao is to have grasped the purpose of being human.

pages 80–81
Tao or God (Ultimate Reality) makes little distinction among people in the experience of the natural world. This may seem indifference, but perhaps it is just space for things to be worked out of their own accord, by

their own nature. The laws of justice and mercy assert their jurisdiction within, whether or not reflected without.

pages 82–83

Though we may be called to pass judgment on people at every turn in the course of our daily lives, a higher truth tells us such activity is folly. Of all the things that are tenuously known in this world, what could be more uncertain than a person's inner character or ultimate contribution? Innocence, tolerance, and acceptance prove better tools to employ than harsh moral judgment.

pages 84–85

The silent working of nature's law is more worthy to correct ills than are fallible humans and corrupt society. What we do to the outcast, we do to ourselves. All bad feeling comes back. Punish someone, and you punish yourself. But gratuitous, unfounded mercy is license, out of accord with natural law.

pages 86–87

To turn away from confrontation is the wise way of the secure person. Conflict and strife bring on injury to the spirit, as much in triumph as defeat. Avoiding conflict is possible in most such confrontations, and what gets cracked is nothing, save a false ego. The greater strength consists in resisting the challenge to smash adversaries. Cosmic justice will prevail in most cases without our agency.

pages 88–89

We reject unsavory people all the time in our day-to-day encounters. That's a matter of survival, and is perhaps how it must be. But are others really so different from us? Who does not have a bad side? There are few without a good side. Reject the bad, but dwell on the positive.

pages 90–91

Seeing beyond the world, animosity dissipates—even the seemingly most justified. Although people may appear vile, who can know their hidden motives? We harden ourselves when we reject people, even though it appears easy. The greater the vision, the less prejudice.

pages 92–93

Jesus taught that true repentance must be followed by forgiveness. Thus two hearts are healed. Lao Tzu conveyed a similar thought: Heaven is indeed impartial, as it sides both with the good person who repents and the good person who forgives.

pages 94–95

Christ thought of his disciples as children, as his family—his true brothers and sisters. The silent sage speaks with his heart and weaves a bond of care among his followers. In that way, the inner circle widens to enfold everyone in its good will.

Hypocrisy

pages 98–99

Those who take advantage of all social privilege and prestige are a despicable lot, because their position, in one way or another, is purchased by the exploitation of others. Somehow they think they are entitled to live this way, that they are superior to those who don't have the inclination to claw and climb up the social hierarchy. The person of wisdom is not taken in by their rank and outer trappings. Indeed, their selfishness and unbridled conceit mark them as objects of disgust, so he chooses to have nothing to do with them.

pages 100–101

Those with a legalistic, rationalistic, or even technical bent of mind are often entrapped in a profound ignorance, no matter how intelligent or knowledgeable they may appear. They usually believe in nothing beyond the world of appearances. They have no use for spiritual concerns, dismissing them as illusory or weakminded. Society values these people highly and rewards them lavishly, but where are their souls? Indeed, they seem to have none. They do not value the teacher of eternal truths, and thus are much gone astray.

pages 102–103

When society grows thoroughly corrupt and spiritually bankrupt, it becomes encased in the tomb of ritual. The dead worshiping the dead.

True movement of the spirit can never come by ritual. It cannot be bribed or extorted. It must arise spontaneously from an upright heart. Thus, ritual and ceremony reveal themselves as fraud—the enemy of meaning. In his obsession with artifice, man turns into gross parody all that is true and natural.

pages 104–105
Deceit is the handmaiden of society. Those who put stock in social convention, legalism, and ritual often add the crown of hypocrisy to their spiritual deadness. Their shallow, complacent attitudes mock the original vision of their tradition. Cut off from heart and soul, they are prone to all manner of social vices. Where once flourished insight and wisdom now stand only shrewdness and cunning.

pages 106–107
The guardians of convention always try to regulate human behavior. And the glue they use to hold society together is falseness. They love to make elaborate rules about what is proper, constructing complex social codes. But when genuine, spontaneous impulses are always stifled, all sorts of social breakdown occurs. So they try to artificially regulate it even more, instead of cultivating inner virtue.

pages 108–109
The social leaders clothe themselves in the finery of their ego. They are full of themselves. Cloaked in "tradition," dripping with wealth and "honor," they have lost sight of all virtue in their passion for privilege. They have vulgarized their own beings. They have insulted God by mocking the equality of man. In all their trappings they appear distinguished, but that is a facile deception. Inwardly they are consumed by an odious disease.

Violence

pages 112–113
Both Lao Tzu and Jesus abhorred violence. Their rejection of war was probably absolute. They used other weapons to conquer people's minds and hearts.

pages 114–115

Lao Tzu and Jesus rejected all manner of violence—psychological as well as physical. They both called for a social experiment to abandon the authoritarian model. They dared to embrace real freedom and equality— no more coercion, no more imposition of will on others. After all, forcing someone to submit to your will is hardly a spiritual practice.

pages 116–117

There shall be no delight in power for power's sake. For that leads to a shadowy area, where the "amoral" shades into the "immoral." The intoxication of victory can be great—even in the name of virtue. Lao Tzu was talking about actual war, and Jesus was talking about a spiritual campaign. Still, the sense is similar. It may be well to delight in the triumph of Good—but the costs should never be forgotten. Do not be seduced by the call of victory—lest you spin out to the side of the darker angels.

pages 118–119

Peace is the way of nature, the working of Tao in the grander vision. Although there is conflict in nature, it exists only in the greater sphere of cooperation. Peace is the prevailing motif. Cataclysm and upheaval, of whatever kind, is an aberration, an "extra-ordinary" event. Artificial cataclysm by armed force is the ultimate folly, producing the most extreme adverse consequences that take generations to heal. To follow the way of peace is to be a child of Tao, blessed of God.

pages 120–121

The symmetry of violence completes itself. Most times the law of cause and effect holds true. Violence as a way of life fulfills itself as a way of death.

Wisdom

pages 124–125

There is a system of harmony and hierarchy at work in the universe. The life force pulses through all, connecting all. There is always a model of natural, perfect being, as close to us as any part of nature. We have only to attune ourselves to it to participate in its perfection.

pages 126–127

Here is a practical test for determining what is true and benevolent. Sometimes it is not so easy to tell. From the origins of something we can have a good idea of its nature. Or as Jesus indicated, you know people's intentions by their actions. Some people say all the right things, but don't follow them. Some don't talk such a good game, but harm no one. Belief and action—both benevolent and malevolent—often go hand in hand. But often they do not. Be clear in discerning the reality beneath the appearance.

pages 128–129

Who has a truly satisfactory answer for tragedy, suffering, and evil? We can surmise some things, spin theories of others, hold to intuitions, or cleave to faith. Occasionally we may get a glimpse of enlightenment or experience an epiphany. But there is so much we cannot know on this earthly level—it is simply beyond our present understanding. These two great traditions, Taoism and Christianity, wisely allow room for that.

pages 130–131

Sweet Jesus wasn't always so sweet! Neither Lao Tzu, the gentle Taoist sage. Or, of course, life itself. Sometimes, in the service of truth, sentiment is swept aside. The higher vision may appear heartless because there is difficult work to be done. Seeking truth is sometimes demanding, a harsh course to traverse, filled with obstacles and constraints that you must overcome. This may involve heartbreak. A certain toughness, even icy detachment, is necessary to pass through this world, the crucible of truth.

pages 132–133

Jesus had a keener sense of evil than Lao Tzu, who saw this issue in more ambiguous tones. Still, Lao Tzu acknowledged that evil abounds when Tao is forgotten, and that evil loses much of its power when Tao is remembered. In his healing, Jesus took on the "evil" of torment from the demon of illness. Jesus aligned himself with virtue and rebuked the demon—banishing its power and preventing it from doing further harm. Thus he helped God or Tao to be remembered in the world.

pages 134–135

The only teaching of value is the lesson that shines from within to instruct without. To teach virtue, be virtuous. To inspire courage, be courageous. To promote faith, be faithful. A healer who abuses his own body impoverishes his own skill. A teacher who has no love for his subject is a cracked vessel. A preacher who ignores his own wisdom is a sack of straw. If you would let the mouth speak, take care that it is nourished by the heart.

pages 136–137

The building of character is the noblest of endeavors. Vanquishing faults and promoting growth through wisdom should be the supreme challenge in life. Domination over the external world, be it in the social, political, or economic realm, is a gross charade of this inner campaign.

pages 138–139

Jesus before Pilate is a dramatic example of *wu-wei*, or the Taoist concept of taking no action. Jesus the meek, the exemplar of softness, questioned by the harsh governor and accused by the spiteful elders. He took almost no action to save himself, and at this point taught with no words. Perhaps Jesus simply had to die for the whole grand scheme of things. Or perhaps trying to save his own life was pointless by then. For he knew a much greater triumph lay ahead for this fallen, hard-hearted world—the Resurrection, the spreading of the Good News, and the day of Divine Judgment. The softest substance does overcome the hardest.

pages 140–141

In the comfort and peace of truth shall you rest. People are drawn to the one who is drawn to the One. Through the ages, in the saints and sages of east and west, there have been many such. Some were known to history; many more remain unknown. The major lights from the East we call Krishna, Buddha, Lao Tzu. In the West, the greatest we call Christ.

pages 142–143

Lao Tzu pointed the way to a life lived in harmony with nature—one of simplicity and integrity. It is a broad path, easy to tread. In the West, Jesus taught by example and embodied such a life. That's why the Gospel of John says that he is the way, the truth, and the life. Should it really be so difficult to follow the true way, rather than get side-tracked on all the lesser paths?

pages 144–145

Those whose vision transcends the world often feel out of place in it. This world is not their true home. It feels like exile, purgatory, hence such people feel homesick and lonely passing through it. They live above the banal and thus are excluded from the comforts of belonging. We should allow them their occasional indulgence in self-pity.

pages 146–147

We are bounded, finite creatures—full of limitations. Therefore it is difficult for us to conceive of something unbounded, infinite, limitless. But drawing on the gifts of intuition, imagination, or faith, we can get an inkling of something beyond our circumscribed consciousness, to which our limitations don't apply. Hence, what appears beyond possibility to our earthbound minds is as nothing to the Unbounded Mind, what we call God or Tao.

pages 148–149

Excessive concern with self will prove counterproductive. "Self-consciousness" regarding either the body or the spirit impedes the spontaneity that keeps things functioning smoothly and naturally. Follow the promptings of an unspoiled heart and all other concerns will fade, along with their attendant vexations.

pages 150–151

Perseverance and perspective are universal virtues, universal truths. Therefore it is not surprising that Lao Tzu and Jesus both spoke to them in their own ways. The most daunting task must begin with a single, initial effort. Then we build from there. Through whatever setbacks and hardships we face, somehow we must resist the temptation to quit. The greatest human task is salvation. It may be an intense struggle, filled with pain and denial—the overcoming of many obstacles. Or it may be far easier under happier circumstances. Or more likely, some mixture of the two. Whatever destiny, we must follow it through to its natural end.

Mysticism

pages 154–155

In these passages, the source of the universe is hinted at in terms of its feminine or nurturative principle. Lao Tzu's "mother of all things" and John's Logos or Word (to become the incarnate Christ) evoke the gentler aspect of the primal mystery. It is divine, nonpersonal love, unable to be differentiated because to do so would be to fragment and diminish it. Still, it is eternal, immutable, ineffable, unknowable—a dynamic mystery from which everything draws being.

pages 156–157

Tao is a hierarchical concept—with different dimensions of manifestation. The Cosmic Tao corresponds to God the Father in the Christian vision—remote, unknowable, impervious—while *Teh*, the animating principle that runs through all life, shaping all movement, corresponds to the Son, the incarnation of the cosmic mystery, taking on form in the natural world. As such, *Teh*, or the Son, is more readily comprehensible since it is closer to our experience. The Father is the remote source of all, but it is channeled through the Son, through whom the world came into being.

pages 158–159

At the intersection of the beginning and the end, time and the timeless, *Teh* returns to Tao and Son returns to Father. Worldly perception blurs, distinction is obliterated, and the Source and its manifestations are revealed as one.

pages 160–161

The natural world—the heart-delighting beauty of creation—can be a window to give us a glimpse of God. We can know something of the Father through the beauty of his handiwork and design. For on one level, as the poet Keats asserted, "Truth is Beauty and Beauty is Truth."

pages 162–163

In the midst of changes and swirling cycles, the heart of being doesn't change. Just as there is unity behind diversity, so too there is immutability beyond flux. Nature is forever transforming, but her laws are eternal. There is a stillness in the heart of turmoil.

Power need not be showy. Most of the time nature is calm and quiet—yet still very powerful. Jesus himself was a force of nature, calm and quiet much of the time—even sleeping through a storm. Yet the power he called forth was sufficient to calm the raging storm, as he calmed the raging anxieties of his disciples, even as they wondered about who was this captain of the universe.

It is the highest wisdom to leave some things to mystery. And the nature of reality is the greatest mystery. Know what you can know, but don't assert more than you can know. Respect the mystery; savor its subtle truth. It is too alive to reduce to categories, too mercurial to pin down. It is something too big to possess. Only a fool or a liar would try.

Shake a bowl of water and after all the agitation, it will revert to calm. There is a dynamic dance ingrained in the nature of things. Everything proceeds in a rhythmic fashion. And within those rhythms are seasons and cycles. All that exists is alive and in flux, from the music of the spheres to the music of our emotions. Learn to dance to that music, matching music to movement, and you'll have mastered much of the artistry of life.

An image of fishing too powerful to resist. The Taoist point is that ultimately all things will balance out, heaven misses nothing—however unlikely that may appear, like fishing with wide nets. A similar drama played out with Jesus and his disciples. Jesus cast his net wide, and caught two very humble, unpromising fishermen to be his first disciples. And against all odds, they grew into revered saints. Heaven's net is indeed wide!

A sense of unity and wholeness pervades your soul when you return to the Source. The great Tao flows everywhere—inside and outside you—and the kingdom does likewise. When you flow in the Tao or when the kingdom takes hold in your heart, God and the world merge.

Immortality

pages 176–177

One of the great questions in life is whether there is or isn't an eternal dimension to the human person. Lao Tzu and Jesus both taught there is. Whether we refer to it as soul, spirit, consciousness, or even energy, to the intuitive it seems nearly self-evident that there is a part of us that is not subject to death. The mind and the body are married in life, but at death do they part.

pages 178–179

Spiritual power sometimes manifests in the world as the ability to transcend danger. Sometimes spiritual power simply means transcending the material world and its evils by cultivating the deathless part of yourself.

pages 180–181

Life in the material world is often hard—why should we fear release from it? Perhaps one reason for the presence of evil and suffering in the world is to make it easier for us to take leave of it. To be too attached to the body is not a good thing: It is another form of materialism. This is a fine balancing act—to love and affirm life, yet to know its worldly end is ultimately of little consequence. The inner life—the world without end—should be our primary concern.

pages 182–183

In the world, sensitive, gentle, guileless people often have a tough time of it. The world doesn't seem to appreciate them much. And in the worst cases, it beats them up pretty good. But that is not necessarily the end of the story. With the right tools, spiritual people can overcome the world—both while still in it and beyond.

pages 184–185

The prime teachings of gentleness, humility, and integrity should not be so difficult to live. They should arise spontaneously from an innocent, benevolent nature. And yet such virtues are exceedingly rare in the world. The sages have given their testimony and model, yet their teachings are merely given lip service while civil society pursues its program of exploitation and consumption. Why is this so? There appears something very wrong with the world, that it is truly fallen. But we need not fall with it. Follow the masters through it and beyond it.

pages 186–187

Lao Tzu's way and Jesus' way were simple and similar. Yet so few people are inclined to follow them. That's why the gate is narrow and the reason Lao Tzu is "distinguished," being something rare. The way need not be so narrow or lonely. It's just that so many people cling to a low level of consciousness. They don't try to free themselves from the clutches of a life mired in ignorance. Don't be one of them.

pages 188–189

The tragedy of the innocent seems to be a drama ingrained in the texture of life. The world often functions like a crucible. Wisdom and virtue, misunderstood, are scorned and vilified. But still, within that tragedy may be revealed a divine meaning. Dignity, strength, and vision will prevail over trial. That is the mission of greatness: the promise beyond, its fulfillment.

Bibliography

Holy Bible, New Revised Standard Version with Apocrypha. New York: Oxford University Press, 1989.

The Wisdom of Laotse, translated, edited and with an introduction and notes by Lin Yutang. New York: Random House, Inc. 1948.

Lao Tsu: Tao Te Ching, translated by Gia-Fu Feng and Jane English. New York: Vintage Books, 1972.

Suggested Reading

Armstrong, Karen. *A History of God.* New York: Ballantine Books, 1993.

Blofeld, John. *Taoism: The Road to Immortality.* Boulder, Co.: Shambala Publications, Inc., 1978.

———. *Taoist Mysteries and Magic.* Boulder, Co.: Shambala Publications, Inc., 1973.

Cooper, J. C. *Taoism: The Way of the Mystic.* Wellingborough, England: Aquarian Press, 1972.

Keating, Thomas. *Open Mind, Open Heart.* Warwick, N.Y.: Amity House, 1986.

Kung, Hans, and Julia Ching. *Christianity and the Chinese Religions.* New York: Doubleday, 1988.

Liu, Da. *The Tao and Chinese Culture.* New York: Shocken Books, 1979.

Magee, John B. *Religion and Modern Man: A Study of the Religious Meaning of Being Human.* New York: Harper & Row, 1967

Merton, Thomas. *Mystics and Zen Masters.* New York: Delta, 1961.

Parrinder, Geoffrey, editor. *World Religions: From Ancient History to the Present.* New York: Facts On File, 1971.

Smith, Huston. *The Religions of Man.* New York: Harper & Row, 1958.

Smullyan, Raymond M. *The Tao Is Silent.* San Francisco: HarperSanFrancisco, 1977.

Watts, Alan. *Tao the Watercourse Way.* New York: Pantheon Books, 1975.

Other Seastone Titles

EINSTEIN AND BUDDHA: THE PARALLEL SAYINGS
Thomas J. McFarlane, Editor   Introduction by Wes Nisker
Einstein and Buddha reveals how modern science and ancient Eastern thought lead
us to the same deep truths. *Hardcover. $19.00*

THE GOSPEL OF THOMAS:
UNEARTHING THE LOST WORDS OF JESUS
John Dart and Ray Riegert   Introduction by John Dominic Crossan
Details the discovery of the greatest collection of apocryphal Christian docu-
ments ever found. The dramatic narrative history is combined with an annotated
translation of The Gospel of Thomas. *Trade paper. $11.95*

JESUS AND BUDDHA: THE PARALLEL SAYINGS
Marcus Borg, Editor   Introduction by Jack Kornfield
Traces the life stories and beliefs of Jesus and Buddha, then presents a compre-
hensive collection of their remarkably similar teachings on facing pages. *Trade
paper. $14.00*

JESUS AND MUHAMMAD: THE PARALLEL SAYINGS
Joey Green, Editor   Foreword by Dr. Sayyid M. Syeed
Introduction by Dr. Richard Atkinson
Presents for the first time—placed side by side—parables of Jesus and the par-
allel ethical teachings of Muhammad. *Trade paper. $14.00*

BUDDHA IN YOUR BACKPACK:
EVERYDAY BUDDHISM FOR TEENS
Franz Metcalf
Especially written for teens, *Buddha in Your Backpack* explains Buddhism and shows
how Buddha's teachings can add a little wisdom and sanity to their high-velocity
lives. *Trade paper. $12.95*

THE LOST GOSPEL Q: THE ORIGINAL SAYINGS OF JESUS
Marcus Borg, Editor   Introduction by Thomas Moore
The sayings within this book represent the very first Gospel. Here is the original
Sermon on the Mount, the Lord's Prayer and Beatitudes. Reconstructed by bib-
lical historians, Q provides a window into the world of ancient Christianity. *Trade
paper. $11.95*

MUSIC OF SILENCE: A SACRED JOURNEY THROUGH THE HOURS OF THE DAY

David Steindl-Rast and Sharon Lebell   *Introduction by Kathleen Norris*

A noted Benedictine monk shows us how to incorporate the sacred meaning of monastic life into our everyday world by paying attention to the "seasons of the day" and the enlivening messages to be found in each moment. *Trade paper. $12.00*

THE TAO OF THE JUMP SHOT:
AN EASTERN APPROACH TO LIFE AND BASKETBALL

John Fitzsimmons Mahoney   *Introduction by Bill Walton*

Much more than a book about basketball, *The Tao of the Jump Shot* describes how to move with grace, prize every action and experience the beauty of life through the simple act of getting a ball through a hoop. *Trade paper. $9.95*

THE UDDHAVA GITA: THE FINAL TEACHING OF KRISHNA

Swami Ambikananda Saraswati, Translator   *Introduction by Thomas Cleary*

Offers the reader philosophy, poetry, guidance and the hope for more complete consciousness. *Trade paper. $14.95*

WHAT WOULD BUDDHA DO?:
101 ANSWERS TO LIFE'S DAILY DILEMMAS

Franz Metcalf

Much as the "WWJD?" books help Christians live better lives by drawing on the wisdom of Jesus, this "WWBD?" book provides advice on improving your life by following the wisdom of another great teacher—Buddha. Not just for Buddhists, *WWBD?* is for anyone looking for spiritual direction and help in navigating through contemporary society. *Trade paper. $9.95*

To order these titles or other Seastone books call 800-377-2542 or 510-601-8301, e-mail ulysses@ulyssespress.com or write to Ulysses Press, P.O. Box 3440, Berkeley, CA 94703. There is no charge for shipping on retail orders. California residents must include sales tax. Allow two to three weeks for delivery.

MARTIN ARONSON, editor of this volume, has devoted much of the past 25 years to studying and practicing Taoism, Christianity, Zen and Tibetan Buddhism, and Sufism. He has lived in several religious communities and currently resides in the San Francisco Bay Area.

BROTHER DAVID STEINDL-RAST, O.S.B., author of the introduction, is a Benedictine monk and the author of *A Listening Heart, Gratefulness: The Heart of Prayer, Music of Silence* (Ulysses Press) and *Belonging to the Universe*, which he co-wrote with Fritjof Capra. He lives in Big Sur, California.